CLASH
by ticktock

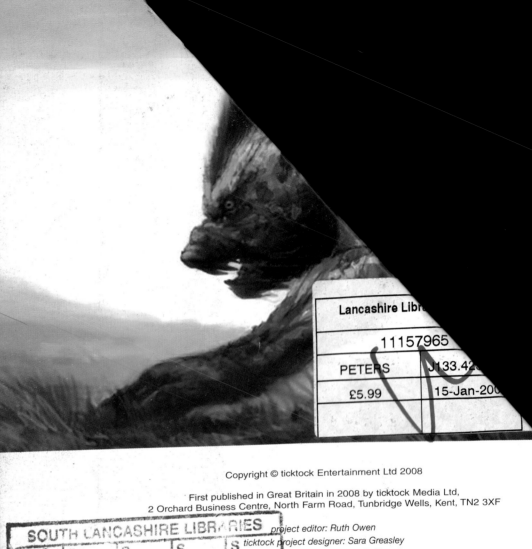

Copyright © ticktock Entertainment Ltd 2008

First published in Great Britain in 2008 by ticktock Media Ltd,
2 Orchard Business Centre, North Farm Road, Tunbridge Wells, Kent, TN2 3XF

project editor: Ruth Owen
ticktock project designer: Sara Greasley
ticktock picture researcher: Lizzie Knowles

With thanks to series editors Honor Head and Jean Coppendale.

Thank you to Lorraine Petersen and the members of nasen

ISBN 978 1 84696 746 7 pbk

Printed in China

A CIP catalogue record for this book is available from the British Library.

Picture credits (t=top; b=bottom; c=centre; l=left; r=right):
Age fotostock/SuperStock: 14. American Werewolf Inc/RGA: 1Christopher Robbins/Getty Images: 22.
Corbis/SuperStock: 18. Pictorial Press Ltd./Alamy: 7, 26, 27bl, 27 br. Mary Evans Picture Library/Alamy: 15t.
The Beast of Gévaudan, published by Basset, 1764 by French School, Musee Nat. des Arts et Traditions Populaires,
Paris, France/ Archives Charmet/ The Bridgeman Art Library. Illustration by Paul Mudie: OFC, p9. ShutterStock: 4-5,
12-13, 14, 15b, 16-17, 19, 20, 21, 23, 24, 25, 28, 31. Tao-Chuan Yeh/AFP/Getty Images: 29.
ticktock Media Archive: 2-3. Steve Gorton/Getty Images: 22.

Every effort has been made to trace copyright holders, and we apologise in advance for any omissions. We would be
pleased to insert the appropriate acknowledgments in any subsequent edition of this publication.

CONTENTS

WEREWOLVES

For thousands of years, people have told stories.

Terrifying stories of beasts that are half human and half wolf.

Stories of
werewolves...

WEREWOLF ATTACK

The night is very dark.
There are shadows everywhere.
You are all alone in the woods.

Suddenly the clouds part.
A full moon shines through
the trees.

A chilling howl fills the night.

You hear a snarl behind you.
You feel hot breath on the
back of your neck.

You turn.

You see dripping fangs shining
in the moonlight.

The fangs sink into your flesh.

There's no escape...

A TERRIFYING CHANGE

Something terrifying is happening. Thick hair starts to grow all over your body.

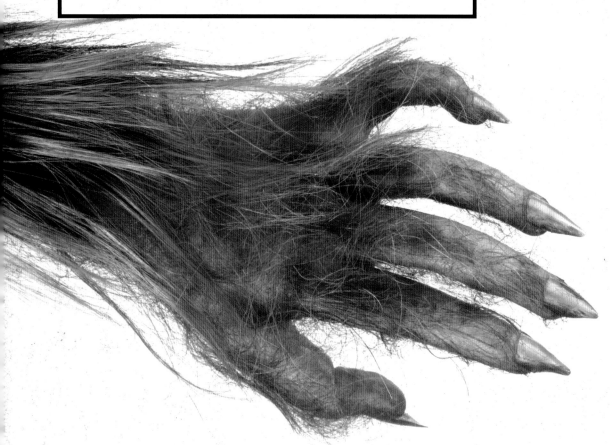

Claws grow from your toes and fingers.

You throw back your head and...

...howl!

Now you have
become a werewolf.
You are doomed
to hunt for flesh
and blood.

9

WILD WOLVES

Of course, a human can't really turn into a wolf. So how did these stories start in the first place?

No one knows for sure. But stories about werewolves have been told for thousands of years.

In the past, large numbers of wolves lived wild in many places.

Sometimes food was short during bad winters. People had to beware. Hungry wolves might attack a person.

Perhaps people told stories about werewolves because they were afraid of being attacked by a real wolf.

WOLF BITE

Some werewolf stories may have started because of a disease called rabies.

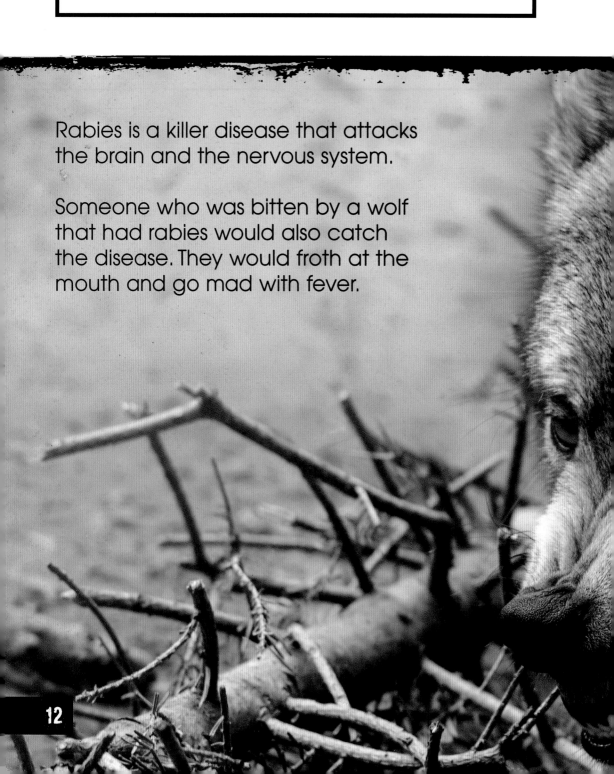

Rabies is a killer disease that attacks the brain and the nervous system.

Someone who was bitten by a wolf that had rabies would also catch the disease. They would froth at the mouth and go mad with fever.

A person with rabies would act like a wild animal!

REAL FEARS

In Viking times, savage warriors, called Berserkers, wore wolf and bearskin cloaks.

In battle, the Berserkers must have looked half human and half animal.

Hundreds of years ago in France, many people believed in werewolves.

Stake

From 1520 to 1630, over 30,000 people were sent to court in werewolf trials. Many people were burnt at the stake for being a werewolf.

Mouldy bread

For some people, the problem was their food. They were very poor and only had mouldy rye bread to eat.

The bread gave them an illness. It made them grunt and shake and their eyes look wild.

A FAMOUS LEGEND

The Beast of Gévaudan is a famous French werewolf legend.

The Beast of Gévaudan was a huge wolf. It killed around 60 people.

The first attack was in 1765. A woman was chased by a wolf in a forest. Luckily, the beast was driven away by farm workers.

This artwork from the time shows the attack.

Other women and children were not so lucky. The wolf dragged them into the forest. It ripped open their necks.

People said the beast
must be a werewolf.

THE BEAST OF GEVAUDAN

Men hunted for the beast. They killed many wolves, but the attacks didn't stop.

After three years of attacks, one hunter finally came face to face with the beast.

The hunter was named Jean Chastel. The legend says that Jean was praying.

When he looked up...

...he saw the beast!

Jean shot the beast through the heart with one silver bullet.

The body of the huge wolf was carried through the town of Gévaudan to show it was dead. But legend says it was not the body of the real beast.

The real body had to be hidden. It was too terrible for people to see.

It looked too human!

HOW TO BECOME A WEREWOLF

In the past, people believed there were many ways to become a werewolf.

A bite from a wolf or a werewolf was one way.

People also believed you would become a werewolf if you were born on a Friday under a full moon. Or, if you slept with the full moon shining on your face.

Some people believed you would be a werewolf if you had six older brothers and sisters.

The seventh child was cursed!

Another belief was that if you drank water from the footprint of a wolf, it would turn you into a werewolf.

HOW TO SPOT A WEREWOLF

Old stories say there are ways to spot a werewolf.

A person who is a werewolf may have fingers that are all the same length.

They might have hair on the palms of their hands...

...or hair inside their ears!

Stories say that a person who is a werewolf may have eyebrows that join in the middle.

They will also love eating raw meat!

HOW TO STOP A WEREWOLF

Old stories tell of ways to make a werewolf turn back into a human.

You can stab it three times in its head with a knife.

Try to get three drops of its blood. When the blood falls to the ground, the werewolf turns back into a human.

A poisonous plant called wolfsbane was said to keep werewolves away.

Maybe the stories started because people saw wolves die if they ate this plant.

Wolfsbane flowers

However, some people believed that eating wolfsbane could turn you into a werewolf.

Werewolf stories say that the only way to kill a werewolf is with a silver bullet.

MOVIE WEREWOLVES

Most of us know about werewolves because of horror movies.

In 1981, a movie called *An American Werewolf in London* came out.

In the movie, two Americans, Jack and David, are attacked by a savage beast.

David's bones and muscles bend and change shape.

Jack is killed. David is bitten, but he lives.

However, on the next full moon, David undergoes a terrible change. Movie-goers had not seen such a terrifying change from human to werewolf before.

Special effects make-up artist Rick Baker won an Oscar for his work on the movie.

His jaw grows longer.

Hair grows all over his body.

REAL-LIFE WOLFMEN

Some werewolf stories may have started because of rare medical conditions.

Some people suffer from a mental illness called lycanthropy.

Lycanthropy makes people believe they have turned into a wolf.

Some people are covered in long hair. They even have hair on their face and hands!

This extreme hairiness is caused by a condition called hypertrichosis.
The word means "extra hair".

This is Jesus Fajardo Aceves from Mexico. He has hypertrichosis. Other members of his family also have the condition. But none of them, of course, is really a werewolf.

NEED TO KNOW WORDS

cursed To have harm wished on you, like a bad spell.

fangs Long, sharp teeth. Predator animals use their fangs to grab, hold and tear apart the animals they hunt.

froth To produce lots of foamy, bubbly spit.

full moon A round moon that appears once a month.

legend A story from the past. Legends cannot be checked or proved.

medical condition An illness or something unusual that affects the body.

mental illness An illness of the brain.

predator An animal that hunts, kills and eats other animals.

rabies A deadly disease passed on by the bite of an animal. Years ago, rabies affected lots of wild animals. Today, the disease is rare.

rare Something that doesn't happen very often.

special effects Tricks that movie-makers use to make something seem real in a movie.

Viking A warrior from hundreds of years ago. The Vikings invaded parts of Europe 1,200 to 900 years ago. They came from Norway, Denmark and Sweden.

werewolf A creature that is half human and half wolf. In Old English the word "were" means "man". So werewolf means "manwolf".

WERE-CREATURES

- Stories of half animal and half human creatures are told all around the world.

- In places where there are no wolves, stories of other dangerous, predator animals are told.

- In stories from Africa, people turn into crocodiles or hyenas. In old stories from China, people turn into tigers. In Japan, they have stories of werefoxes. In Russia, stories are told about werebears!

READ MORE ONLINE

Websites

http://www.everythingwolf.com/wolftalk.aspx
Hear real-life wolf howls and learn about wolf conservation

http://www.parentinghumor.com/activityecenter/jokes/werewolf.htm
Werewolf jokes

INDEX